RELAXED ELEGANCE

RIZZOLI
NEW YORK

New York Paris London Milan

RELAXED ELEGANCE

ROOMS FOR LIVING WELL

BRITTANY BROMLEY

WITH KATHRYN O'SHEA-EVANS

To Mimsy, Poppy, and Alexandra, who never thought
this book was a matter of *if* but always *when*.
And to Charlotte and Gigi,
who have made this life so very beautiful.

CONTENTS

INTRODUCTION

I've always known that I was a designer. As a child, I was much more interested in Barbie's Dreamhouse than I was in Barbie herself. But it was so much more than Mattel. We lived in a brownstone that dated back to 1888, and my brother and I would make elaborate maps of where in the house we imagined treasures and secret passageways might be located. His cartography was always very direct—a series of rectangular rooms, arranged in grids—whereas mine almost always included architectural flourishes and *all* of the furniture—an early indicator of my passion for a good floor plan.

I was fortunate to grow up in a family where beautiful interiors were a crucial component of a life well-lived. Our Chicago brownstone and pied-à-terre in New York—where my father traveled often for business—were aesthetically dynamic and important. That was just as true outside; my mother is a master gardener, and she made the grounds surrounding our homes extremely lovely.

Because of that familial affection for design, I spent a lot of my time in antique stores from a young age. One of my earliest childhood memories is going to one with my parents. They gave me a package of Necco Candy Buttons—dots of rainbow confections that need to be peeled individually from a long roll of paper before you eat them—and informed me that we would be at the store until I finished eating them. Now that I'm a parent myself, I realize this was great strategic planning; it kept me occupied so long that I remember thinking that I might grow old and die there. But my parents emerged from their spree with a very nice piece—an English George III sideboard in flame mahogany dating from 1790—that still lives in their home in Chicago.

Moments like this taught me the importance of timeless choices, and I've taken that wisdom with me as I've developed my own style. It's epitomized by the title of this book: *Relaxed Elegance*. Like my parents, who installed a sisal rug, long before it was popular, in our family room replete with Pierre Frey fabrics and decoratively painted strié walls, I favor spaces that are considered and collected but not stuffy. I want my

home to reflect my taste, travels, and lifestyle but not in a way that feels pretentious or contrived. Case in point: to keep the treillage that is layered over antique silver-backed paper on the walls of my family room from feeling too formal, I paired it with a simple, striped cotton dhurrie underfoot.

I find that I can always envision new ways of doing things; I don't need to see a rendering before I jump. I also love color. I don't require it in abundance, but understanding color—which hues work together, and what dynamic they create—helps us create spaces that are wholly original. Every room should have personality, and the pieces within them should have their own stories to tell. That is why we often choose antiques and vintage pieces that have unusual turns of leg or a little bit of wear. To me, that patina makes something more beautiful—not less. And it perfectly defines what I mean when I say "relaxed elegance."

I championed that concept even in my first profession, as a residential real estate broker in Manhattan, when I often suggested to clients how they might improve a space or visualize layouts. Later, when we scooped up our first home in Bedford, New York (then a weekend escape), neighbors saw how I had decorated and asked if I could assist them with their own interiors—and the rest is history.

Since founding Brittany Bromley Interiors—based in Bedford and now with a second location in Palm Beach, Florida—I've been very fortunate to have clients who have placed enough trust in us that we've been able to design spaces that are both traditional and unexpected and that are very much reflective of their lives and experiences. I adore working with our clients, and I believe that it's a real privilege to help people form the backdrops for the memories that they will create. Every home we design embodies the people who live there, rather than my personal taste. At BBI, our team always says that the only home that you get to decorate like it's yours is your own home.

Years after I began this journey, I still feel I have the best job in the world. I truly believe that if you love what you do, you'll never work a day in your life. You'll find many of my decorating lessons in the pages of this book, but one rule reigns above them all: when spaces are designed and tailored to be true to the souls who live there, every house is a Dreamhouse.

CHAPTER ONE

BUILT TO LAST

I looked at our home in Bedford, New York, with no fewer than fifteen different contractors before we decided to make an offer on it. Every single one of them told me: "Don't walk. Run. This house will be a money pit." But two facts made me ignore them. One, I'm apparently quite stubborn. And two, I just loved her. How could I not? Set on five acres, the property is a historic landmark here in Bedford: a gracious colonial center hall built in 1790—the same year revolution was aswirl in France. She was, it was true, suffering from a serious case of benign neglect. The intervening years had not been kind to her, and decades of deferred maintenance had taken their toll. However, as soon as we gave her the attention she deserved, the house immediately felt happier. By that I mean there was a shift in the ether, a feeling of contentment and an almost audible exhale of relief. Designers often call their own homes their design laboratories, and in this instance, there were no limits on my creativity (except for perhaps budgetary constraints!).

When we took ownership, the house exterior was a deep tan—a color I would refer to as "Baby's First Solids." We painted it Benjamin Moore Chalk White, bumping it up 15 percent with additional gray pigment to get our shutter color and another 15 percent for the door—sorcery that gave her a subtle but beguiling contrast. We then installed slabs of antique granite as doorsteps, which happen

An eighteenth-century hutch from a French boulangerie felt instantly at home in our entrance hall, as if it was custom-made for the space and to house our antique silver.

to be the exact height one needs to mount a horse. (Historical integrity is always appreciated, especially in a landmarked house!) The previous kitchen felt very similar to Grey Gardens, with a plexiglass window insulated around the edges with tinfoil and a range tucked within a 1970s McDonald's-style brick opening. It also had the lowest ceilings in the house, a fact that I embraced by painting much of the cabinetry a rich sooty black. For elegance, I installed Calacatta Viola marble counters and Pierre Frey silk wallpaper. To add depth, I put in mercury glass backsplashes. (They are now commercially available but did not exist at that time, and to get the effect that I'd been dreaming about, I had to use acid etching material and age the plate glass pieces by hand—it's a long story.) I replaced faulty sliding glass doors with multiple pairs of French doors to allow access to the whitewashed brick terrace and gardens from the kitchen and formal living and family rooms, letting the spaces feel more European.

I was intent on preserving the home's original wood floors, which alternate between 12½ and 9½ inches wide—common in the eighteenth century when old-growth, locally sourced lumber was abundant in the surrounding areas.

PREVIOUS PAGE: Painting the exterior in varying shades of Benjamin Moore Chalk White highlights its architecture while giving it a seamless and calm effect.
OPPOSITE: I enlisted decorative painter Mary Meade Evans to paint the original floors of our 1790 colonial center hall in Bedford in a checkerboard pattern— an age-old look that also feels modern, thanks to its graphic quality.

This front hallway runs the full length to the back of the house, so it's a real moment when you open the front door. The light fixture above is Juliska. The ceilings aren't incredibly high, so we chose something that would retreat and create an airy effect.

Dining rooms are opportunities for unbridled grandeur: a place that should delight the eye as much as the palate.

Plank width notwithstanding, they were dry, brittle, and very red. So I stained and resealed them in a midlevel brown that wouldn't provide as much color feedback. In the entryway, on top of this newly neutral base, I had my decorative painter paint a classic checkerboard in cream in a translucent finish that is not entirely opaque, leaving the wood grain visible.

The front door is also original. I was determined to reveal her inner beauty, so I bought a heat gun and spent countless hours peeling off nine generations of what I suspect was lead paint to get down to the original wood and uncover the elegant proportions of the millwork. That little project likely obliterated more of my brain cells than I care to admit, but it was worth it; underneath, the jamb and sidelights were all one piece, and they all still had their original period glass. Bringing to bear an additional historical gravitas to the entryway is an eighteenth-century French bakery hutch (now stocked with a horde of silver in lieu of the day's pastries). I also combined two different ribbons with a hot glue gun to create flat-panel bows on which to hang John Gould bird prints, further to my design ethos: if you can't find what you want for sale, make it.

My dear friends who own Casa Gusto in Palm Beach, Florida, helped me create my newly imagined dining room, where I envisioned three-dimensional florals and trees capable of articulated movement reminiscent of a tree of

Adorning our dining room in papier-mâché up to the faux-tiled ceiling gave it a poetic quality worthy of verse, especially when paired with the silk table skirt complete with a ruffle, but the woven jute rug brings it all down to earth. We also added a ceiling beam to echo the existing ones in the kitchen so the adjacent rooms would speak to one another.

Made by my friends at Casa Gusto, the papier-mâché details in our dining room are meant to evoke the ageless pattern of the tree of life. Note the reproduction medallion at right, which illuminates beautifully at night. The faux bois framing in the background adds a hint of rusticity.

ABOVE: A row of antique John Gould prints parades down our stairway. I custom-made the ribbon mounts using two ribbons and plenty of hot glue. OPPOSITE: Our dog, Banksy, enjoys the fruits of my obsession with down-filled cushions in the living room.

PREVIOUS PAGES: All decorators have an itch they want to scratch. For me, it was this Bennison silk floral fabric. ABOVE: I brought the Louis XV bergère into the present day with an animal print upholstery. OPPOSITE: To give our living room a feminine feel with an edge, I developed a custom peach color for the walls and had our decorative painter, Mary Meade Evans, paint the floors to emulate the parquet at Versailles. Only the zebra rug interrupts the pattern.

This corner banquette provides extra seating when we're entertaining; I especially love the silk trim on the pillows, which is from Décor de Paris and so soft we call it "the Caterpillar." There is hardly any overhead light in my entire house, which is fine by me; we joke that before the invention of the Pico switch smart remote, it took me twenty-seven minutes to turn off every lamp in the house by hand. I felt like the old woman carrying the candle in the dish!

28

Portieres not only provide privacy between spaces but also supply a graceful softness.

life motif. They fabricated all the panels off-site, tailored to the room's specifications—no easy feat in a truly "settled" home where there's a six-inch floor level difference from one side of the room to the other! Now, every surface in the room is papier-mâché, including the faux-tiled ceiling. It feels historical, which was exactly my aim, such that it would feel grounded in a sense of place and time. A nineteenth-century French garden cart, ruffled silk table skirt, and French chairs upholstered in faux alligator fabric finish the space. Although it may appear precious, it's not; we really use this room, and my daughters and I often pile on the sofa with our dog, Banksy, all of us basking in the pretty afternoon light that filters through the papier-mâché vines that climb the window frames.

In the primary suite, my talented, and saintly, mother helped me hand paint the antique French headboard the perfect aged Swedish blue gray, which serves as a counterpoint to the striped canopy above. The wallcovering is actually a Bennison fabric, which I adored so much that I had it paper-backed in order to hang it as a wallpaper. It's the ideal backdrop for another love of mine: antique oil paintings, for which I have a weakness and therefore a constantly evolving collection. In pride of place above the mantel hangs a portrait of what my daughters and I jokingly refer to as my spirit animal, a glamorous woman in a dressing gown perched on a bearskin, with two large Irish hound dogs curled at her feet. I wholeheartedly approve of her life choices, as I hope she does mine.

I wanted this adjoining space to feel both different from and related to our living room. The custom curtains divide the rooms and look beautiful both open and closed, whether you're on the Bennison silk floral side or this green silk gingham side.

PATTERN MIXING

Finding patterns that work well together is a bit like doing the seating chart at a dinner party. You want your guests to have things in common, but you also want their conversations to engage one another and create an almost chemical reaction from which they all benefit. We often begin our design concepts by selecting one multicolored pattern—our "hero" fabric, often a floral—and from there we layer in a geometric, such as a stripe or a check, and then something more organic, like a hand-blocked batik on a coarse-weave linen.

To find out what pairs well together, don't trust what you see online; it's vital to order samples that you can hold in your hands. We used to put samples up on a board, but I find it really helpful to see everything flat on the same table plane. Know that memo samples for multicolored textiles are often quite large so that you can see the repeat of those patterns, but when you're looking at something smaller and hand blocked, they generally only give you a small piece of it, which may not represent the larger pattern. Find images of the fabric on furniture to make sure that you still appreciate the repeating pattern on a larger scale. And just as with dinner party companions, when you're mixing motifs, it goes back to that old adage: if you love it, it will work. I'm sure there are people out there who would say that a marbleized wallpaper with a floral hand-blocked batik and acid-yellow velvet is too much! But for me, it's just right.

OPPOSITE AND ABOVE: Here we started with marbleized wallpaper, which had many colors from which to jump off, and then chose our sofa floral from Lee Jofa and a hand-blocked batik from Jennifer Shorto for the ottoman. Solids in this room act as grounding elements, such as the deep olive green of the millwork.

ABOVE: Ranunculus in different shades of coral are my kryptonite. OPPOSITE: This John Derian for Pierre Frey wallpaper is one of the most beautiful wallpapers I've ever seen; I knew right away I had to have it for my powder room. The French drawer pulls and knobs from P. E. Guerin pop against the black vanity.

PAGE 36: The Calacatta Viola marble is one of my favorite materials for the movement in its veining. PAGE 37: Matchstick blinds supply additional texture in our breakfast nook. The wallpaper is silk from Pierre Frey, and the sconces are French antiques. ABOVE: We retained the sense of history in the kitchen, which has the lowest ceilings in the house, by keeping the exposed original beams intact. OPPOSITE: Nobody looked askance at me when I said I'd be painting the cabinetry and trim black; it hides all manner of sins.

OPPOSITE: We wanted this little sitting area to feel very considered. Grass cloth walls bring such modern warmth, which can be pivotal in a more than two-hundred-year-old house. ABOVE, CLOCKWISE FROM TOP LEFT: Trim details on the leading edge of a curtain. Antiques in inky black always feel modern. I love a pleated shade in a matching fabric. Indigos and sands pair beautifully together.

PREVIOUS PAGES: The family room was the primary bedroom for our home's previous owners, but we reimagined it entirely; we added French doors out to the terrace and had the ceiling sheathed in a reflective Phillip Jeffries wallpaper and then painted in treillage by Mary Meade Evans. ABOVE, CLOCKWISE FROM TOP LEFT: When in doubt, add a ruffle. Layering patterns in similar tones adds richness. A pom-pom edge is wonderfully tactile. A juxtaposing choice of piping highlights the architectural silhouette of a piece. OPPOSITE: Lucite curtain rods add to the open feel.

Antique paintings bring so much to a room: timeless beauty, the glimmer of gilding, and the entrancing aura of generations past.

For the primary bedroom, I had a Bennison fabric paper-backed so that I could hang it as a wallcovering. The headboard is a French antique with a matching pair of footboards; the canopy is attached to the ceiling and adds to the immersive floral feeling.

OPPOSITE: Leaning paintings rather than hanging them can lend a delightful feeling of nonchalance, relaxed elegance personified. ABOVE, CLOCKWISE FROM TOP LEFT: Accessorizing with stripes keeps antique oil paintings from reading as stuffy. Ditsy prints bring so much to a shirred shade. The true meaning of "detail oriented." A neoclassical Empire gilt mirror.

ABOVE: Pierre Frey wallpaper in my daughter's bathroom is whimsical and sophisticated; pairing it with coral prevents the green-on-green space from feeling overly serious. OPPOSITE: The intense green color we chose lives up to her directive: she wanted something mature and a little bit moody.

OPPOSITE: Outside my dressing room, I both camouflaged and played up this hall's existing wood paneling with stripes that run up to a Seussian ceiling. ABOVE: Just off the family room, this pink hallway continues the checkerboard floor of the center hall.

PREVIOUS PAGES: One of the first choices I made in this house was this David Hicks wallpaper in mustard yellow for the nursery. Over the years, we layered in marbleized paper to the backs of the bookcases and brought in Soane Britain chairs. The room feels eclectic and warm. ABOVE AND OPPOSITE: Lacquerware prevents lighter colors from floating away. FOLLOWING PAGES: We re-covered the antique beds from my childhood in a quilted Schumacher fabric for my eldest daughter's room.

OPPOSITE: In my eldest daughter's room, woven baskets supply extra storage for a budding bibliophile's collection under the window seat. ABOVE, CLOCKWISE FROM TOP LEFT: There's a lot of black in this room, which is very strong and very true to my daughter's personality. Canopies soften the stripes. Pierre Frey wallpaper brings an Egyptian touch—and answered her call for tigers on the walls. Generations of my family have dreamed big dreams in these beds.

ABOVE: Klismos chairs bring their timeless elegance to our garden.
OPPOSITE: Limiting the color palette of your plantings—here, whites and varying greens—can help a landscape or a veranda feel especially serene.

ABOVE: Our lush, exultant summers are our reward for New York winters.
OPPOSITE: Accessorizing your outdoor areas is every bit as vital as it is indoors.
For me, flickering lanterns and a flurry of curated custom pillows are key.

—CHAPTER TWO—
A MODERN MIX

The women of New York are famous for turning heads well into their octogenarian years and beyond, and this Park Avenue apartment was no different. The prewar co-op needed some cosmetic updating, but her bones were so gorgeous that most of the project was just an exercise in layering: in other words, we just needed to dress her up a bit!

When I first walked into the space, it felt almost cavernous, thanks to its generous floor plans and high ceilings. Our goal was to create a more intimate feeling and to do so quickly. These long-time clients of mine were a young family and wanted to get settled in their new home as soon as possible, and they needed it to function well on a number of levels. For the adults, it had to be both elegant for formal entertaining and comfortable for Sunday Night Football and mah-jongg. For their growing children, it had to work as a free-range playhouse. Every area needed to serve double, if not triple, functions.

On this project, we had an amazing muse in our clients' contemporary art collection, the hues of which served as jumping-off points for our color palettes. The wife has a very strong aesthetic; she requested that the interiors be soothing and restful but also vibrant. So we walked a very fine line between clean modernity (rare in an apartment of this vintage!) and whimsy, to breathe new life into this very traditional framework.

PAGE 66: We had the floor of the front gallery decoratively painted by Shelly Denning—a graphic touch that juxtaposes beautifully against the Gustavian-era daybed. We went back and forth quite a bit on the pattern to land on the right scale so the clients wouldn't tire of it. ABOVE: White silk walls brought eternal elegance to the living room, but we tempered the fabric with colorful contemporary art, like this piece by Kikuo Saito. OPPOSITE: A duo of symmetrical ferns emphasizes the classic beauty of the newly gleaming cream lacquered woodwork. In the background hangs Cy Twombly's work, *Roman Notes I*, 1970.

Arranged in a grid, a series of contemporary art pieces can be much more impactful and graphic.

The primary way we accomplished this aim was by simultaneously embracing elegance without forsaking a measure of playfulness. One of our first goals was to shine a spotlight on the prewar architecture by lacquering many of the walls, including the front gallery, which spans the length of the apartment and connects the formal dining and living rooms. (As soon as you varnish anything so that it becomes reflective, you emphasize the architecture.) The scale of this space is dramatic, so we kept the palette quiet with glossy cream lacquer on the walls and gold leaf paper on the ceiling for added depth and reflectivity. Underfoot, we had the floor decoratively painted in an abstract geometric pattern, to conjure the classic stone lobbies of such New York architectural icons as the Woolworth Building and the main branch of the New York Public Library. Like the antique Gustavian daybed that we paired with it, it lends gravitas, but the hard-wearing paint and intricate motif handily take a beating from the children's book bags and the like.

At twenty feet by thirty feet, the adjacent living room is expansive, especially by Manhattan standards. We rendered this space formal with white silk walls, but livened it up with bright and colorful fabrics, like Pierre Frey Arty Tapisserie, painted by French abstract artist Marie-Cécile Aptel. The traditional furniture silhouettes were a deliberate mechanism to allow for creativity; when a shape is familiar, you can upholster it in an unexpected pattern and the juxtaposition makes both more compelling. In order to make our silk walls feel less precious,

PREVIOUS PAGES: A simple windowpane-grid upholstery on the armchairs is a calming moment for the eye. This family has an amazing, and constantly growing, contemporary art collection, which helped inspire the color palette. OPPOSITE: The game chairs were influenced by the art deco period—the provenance of the building itself—but we upholstered them in a bold fabric that feels relevant today.

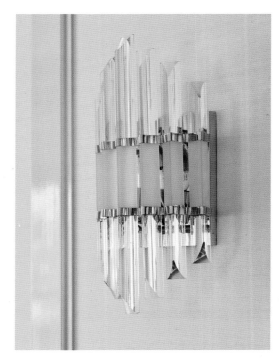

ABOVE, CLOCKWISE FROM TOP LEFT: We're well-known for our custom ottomans with pull-out trivet trays. The mid-century Murano sconces are interesting enough to act as art. Pierre Frey Arty Tapisserie fabric pairs well with solids and graphics alike. Our abaca rug lends plenty of visual charm. OPPOSITE: The feminine silhouette of the Lucite armchairs brings a lovely softness.

We evicted the bookshelves that once lived in this dining room and instead installed elegant paneling that we then lacquered in Farrow & Ball Skylight blue gray. Against it, the paprika-hued chairs supply a punch, but limiting the chevron pattern to the chairbacks means the effect is not too strong.

ABOVE: The Gustavian dining table is essentially a blank canvas—the perfect background for a colorful tablescape. OPPOSITE: A Niermann Weeks chandelier emits an ethereal light; each leaf in the acanthus-like pattern is articulated with multiple glass cylinders.

we paired them with an abaca rug that reads as both a neutral and a geometric. Overhead, pale blue lacquer ceilings call attention to how much light the room gets (and, as a bonus, they make you feel like you're sitting inside an abalone shell). Amid all this, we kept the window treatments fairly simple in embroidered silk. There is a high level of detail up close, but the overall effect is muted, gracious, and ultimately subtle.

One of the largest transformations in this home was the study. It began its life as a rather ho-hum space: it was extremely traditional and presented itself like every stodgy, wood-paneled room throughout history. To highlight the paneling and bookcase elevations, we decoratively painted them in tortoiseshell floor to ceiling. Because the room is visible from the formal gallery through a large set of double doors, we needed a coffee table with an interesting profile. After fruitlessly searching for an antique that would work, we designed our own scalloped piece and had it wrapped in tawny leather. I love how it plays with the chevron velvet tuxedo sofa in crimson and the fine palettes of the floral lampshades and window treatments, both of which act as punctuation marks here. When twilight settles over the city and the lights are low, you almost imagine that you're dashing into the Carlyle for a cocktail and jazz, all from the comfort of your own home.

We love upholstering traditional furniture in unexpected patterns. In this study, the chevron velvet tuxedo sofa has a secret: it's a sleeper sofa. We decoratively painted the room's existing paneling in a tortoiseshell pattern, which transformed it into a jewel box.

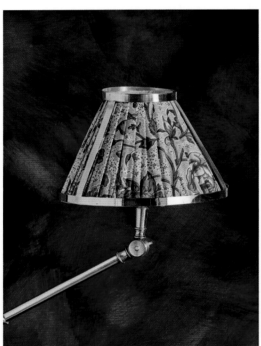

ABOVE, CLOCKWISE FROM TOP LEFT: Leather wrapping the custom coffee table made it both handsome and durable. Lampshades are an excellent way to experiment with patterns in small doses. Crimson velvet and delicate calico are an entrancing juxtaposition. Custom Pierre Frey lampshade. OPPOSITE: The lampshades in the bar were an opportunity for more color, so we opted for a punctuation mark.

ABOVE: The heavily veined marble is visually loud, so we intentionally opted for a quiet cabinetry color, decoratively painted by Shelly Denning with strié. OPPOSITE: We wanted the breakfast nook to feel playful and young; the kitchen table is where you live for the first few years of your children's lives, so you want it to feel happy.

My client loved the bedroom I did for a recent Kips Bay Decorator Show House in Palm Beach, Florida, so much that he asked me to essentially re-create it for their primary. The Italianate armchair is cerused oak.

OPPOSITE: The modern art above the banquette is especially eye-catching and engaging because of its traditional backdrop. Bolsters at either end of the L-shaped seat make it so much more comfortable. ABOVE: A lovely perch for late-night emails is essential.

OPPOSITE: The eldest child shares his father's love of the Chicago Cubs. We wanted his bedroom to feel as handsome as a haberdashery; note the windowpane-grid wool fabric lining the ceiling, inspired by men's suits. ABOVE, CLOCKWISE FROM TOP LEFT: We love to create bedrooms that will stand the test of time as children mature. Woven surfaces provide needed texture. Campaign chest details on the vanity. Stripes recall vintage baseball uniforms.

ABOVE: A small-scale, peach-pink Kathryn Ireland print adorns
the walls of the daughters' room. OPPOSITE: Touches of blue and
aqua help prevent the room from feeling too sweet.

LOVING PINK

ABOVE: Glossy, creamy pink woodwork throughout brings patterns to life. OPPOSITE: Twin bed canopies draw the eye up and help define each daughter's individual space.

It's not difficult to look at my portfolio and see that I truly love the color pink. Maybe it goes back to my early days with the Barbie Dreamhouse! I believe that, as a rule, people undervalue it. It's one of the most complex colors in the color wheel, with so many different shade variations that it's both tricky and satisfying to achieve exactly what you envision. In this room, we wanted a pink that felt feminine but not overly saccharine. So we chose a pink that has a little yellow and even a bit of green to its composition. A blue-toned pink can come across as the color of Pepto Bismol, but this particular shade reads as more of a neutral and doesn't fight with the other colors.

I think pink is a truly sophisticated shade. It also tends to play well with a lot of other colors; you can use it with pastels and pops of brighter shades like turquoise and yellow, or treat it as a neutral and lean into a classic pairing such as chocolate brown. I am also convinced that pink has a superpower: it tends to be a universally flattering color in which everyone appears younger, softer, and generally more beguiling.

CHAPTER THREE

THE GREAT ESCAPE

My clients fell for their weekend home in Pound Ridge, New York, because it looked a bit like an English cottage—its fieldstone walls clad in ivy and Chippendale railings standing at strict attention—and yet it had some of the perks that centuries-old homes tend to lack, including high ceilings and generously sized windows. It helped that the previous owners had terrific taste. The house was already lovely and very "done," but it just wasn't what my clients imagined for themselves. Our mission from the get-go was to layer and warm the spaces, creating a lively setting for their young family's country weekends.

Take the dining room: originally a chilly, subdued blue, I knew immediately that I wanted to reimagine the walls in a warm coral lacquer, and thankfully my clients embraced my vision—one that eventually came to define this space. Coral is a color that changes quite a bit throughout the day depending on the light, so we worked tirelessly to come up with a custom shade that would look as beautiful at eleven o'clock in the morning as it does at eleven at night. We tried six different versions of the color before landing on this hue, a custom mix of Fine Paints of Europe Hollandlac enamel. The ceiling above is rendered in a beautiful creamy lacquer, which is comfortable without seeming stuffy. It's an incredible room in which to host dinner parties because the coral walls make everyone's skin glowing and

PAGE 96: A stone facade is eternally elegant. OPPOSITE: In a living room as generously proportioned as this one, we employed several zones for entertaining and plenty of greenery to echo the lush world beyond the windows. Inky-black furniture legs and accessories help anchor the light color palette.

ABOVE: Skirted tables can soften the effect of a room with ample furniture with legs.
OPPOSITE: A Pierre Frey velvet floral made the sofas so comfortable that it is difficult to leave them.
FOLLOWING PAGES: A classic, symmetrical plan will always be calming to the human eye.

ABOVE, CLOCKWISE FROM TOP LEFT: The only thing better than a Pierre Frey pillow is one with a pom-pom fringe. Inverted silk pleats on the lampshade hold their own against the wallpaper. Our custom ottomans feature pull-out trivet trays for drinks. Coral piping helps pull the adjacent dining room's color palette into the mix so the two spaces speak to each other.
OPPOSITE: At a game table, chairs with casters always win; they're both functional and fun.

A dining room lacquered in a soft coral does every dinner guest a favor by basking them in a warm glow.

dewy—especially in the soft light of the 1930s crystal chandelier sourced from a hôtel particulier in Paris. Everything looks better when enveloped in this color.

We didn't want the house to feel like a period piece, especially because it's not technically historical. One of the first things that we did was stain the existing honey-brown wood floors a darker hue, a custom mix of Jacobean and dark walnut, so that there wasn't too much red, which gives off a ton of color feedback. I chose this particular mixture because it's dark enough to read as a neutral and yet versatile enough to play with all colors, and you can still see the grain of the wood for texture and color variation.

Throughout, we mixed antiques with things that feel fresh and new, such as the custom hand-blocked tablecloth with a very relaxed, large jute braid trim in the dining room. It doesn't feel overly considered and provides a crucial note of relaxed elegance. It is a country home, after all, so it is impor-tant that nothing feels too formal. That's evident in the choices we made in the long hallway where we clad the walls in a neutral, patterned grass cloth and paired an antelope runner with cerused oak chairs. It's also clear in the elements we selected for the room that we affectionately refer to as "the Bar Room," where we mingled hand-blocked batik upholstery with a Regency-era gilt table, glossy gray-blue walls, and soft dusty pinks.

From the very first moment I saw the living room, I knew the floor plan would lend itself beautifully to a double seating area. We used a central linchpin of double sofas, arranged back-to-back, where one portion was designed to be

I've worked with these clients before so they were more readily willing to take a chance on my vision for the dining room: a warm coral in high-gloss enamel. The late 1930s chandelier spent its earliest years in a hôtel particulier in Paris. FOLLOWING PAGES: The lacquered ceiling beautifully reflects the glow of the light fixture.

OPPOSITE: Amid the radiance of the candelabras, wall sconces, and enamel walls, every dinner guest may feel as radiant as an Austen character. ABOVE, CLOCKWISE FROM TOP LEFT: The architecture of the dentil molding comes to the forefront in high gloss. Every petal on the crystal chandelier glimmers after dusk. Stone tabletops can lend functionality to antique pieces. Take tablecloths up a notch with tassel trim.

ABOVE: I bought the Regency-era gilt table in Europe; next to it, hand-blocked batik prevents the wingback chair from feeling stuffy. OPPOSITE: The antique Turkish rug, which swirls with dusky roses and very pretty blues, inspired the color palette of the entire bar. We tucked an antiqued mirror into the back of the bar to increase light and, let's face it, to add glamour. The walls are lacquered in Farrow & Ball Hague Blue.

Ever since picture galleries had pride of place in British manors, hallways have showcased art and *objets*—passed by but never passed over.

more casual, with inviting upholstered pieces and an ottoman in lieu of a coffee table. The other seating area—tailor-made for entertaining around the fireplace—is adorned with a brass table and ebonized chairs inlaid with mother-of-pearl. Because the room isn't symmetrical, we placed the "relaxed" zone within the smaller half of the space and installed a game table in the corner where the family can gather for cards or puzzles. Two silvery, sage-green olive trees flanking the mantel give a nod to the leafy acreage beyond the windows.

Upstairs, the primary bedroom had some interesting angles to its existing walls. We decided to embrace them, sheathing them in a Phillip Jeffries wallcovering made from a wood veneer marquetry inlaid with a gray metallic. We echoed the latter color on the moldings and employed an abstract striped floral fabric I'd been wanting to use forever on the window treatment, headboard, and bolster. The results are so restful and peaceful. I echoed the fanciful lines of the headboard in their son's room, which is tailored to suit his "old soul" personality, including Clarence House Tibet wallpaper and an antique drop-front desk that serves as a bedside table.

Although this couple had young children, they were not afraid of materiality, and there wasn't a moment when they chose not to use something special as a precaution against future mishaps. To that end, we selected an incredible Pierre Frey floral velvet for the double sofas in the living room and mixed in neutrals and warm shades of brown to ground the room. Summer, winter, fall, spring—this space feels layered and inviting all year long.

The previous iteration of this hallway was caramel beige, which wasn't doing it any favors. We sheathed it in Feather Bloom wallpaper by Celerie Kemble for Schumacher, which reads like a batik. The pair of Venetian-style, Italianate cerused oak armchairs feel more playful when upholstered in a ZAK+ FOX batik fleur-de-lis.

CREATURE COMFORTS

One of the most important things to consider when you're designing a bedroom—whether it's a primary or guest suite—is all the functions the space needs to serve. To that end, we always ensure that our bedroom window treatments are capable of indulging a whim for a midday nap with functional blackout lining. I love to include a chaise lounge or a chair on which you can pack a suitcase or place laundry, otherwise you'll end up with everything on the bed. A storage piece is also important, whether you need to have a place to tuck free weights and a yoga mat out of sight or simply to hold daily necessities in an orderly and convenient location.

In general, our bedroom color palettes tend to be of the more serene variety; you won't find a lot of red bedrooms in the BBI portfolio! Lastly, we always make sure that we have adequate reading lamps and generously proportioned bedside tables. You need a place to put your book, a flower arrangement, a glass of water (or even a pitcher), or a phone within easy reach without creating a Jenga effect.

OPPOSITE: The Pierre Frey motif on the headboard, bolster, and window treatments is one of my all-time favorites for its abstract florals and strict stripes. ABOVE: In this contemplative bedroom, we covered the walls with a Phillip Jeffries wall treatment made of wood veneer that's inlaid with metallic marquetry. It was so painstaking to install that when it went up—and went up well—we all breathed a huge sigh of relief.

OPPOSITE: Clarence House Tibet wallpaper suits this child's smart, spunky personality. I bought his bedside table—an antique drop-front desk—in Florida, from the estate of Anne Bass. ABOVE: We knew we wanted a fun, cherry-red side table for the son's room and eventually found the The One: a vintage toy piano. The Schumacher fabric on the reading chair is so thick that it feels like a coverlet.

CHAPTER FOUR

CITY GARDENS

S ometimes, you have to shut the door on "open-plan living." In fact, in certain instances, you may even want to lock it behind you. We did just that in this classic Upper East Side pre-war apartment, where the previous owners had used the dining room as a family room without any separation from the formal living room. That simply didn't suit the needs of my clients, a newly married couple who love to entertain on a frequent and sophisticated scale. The husband is a fabulous chef and talented musician, and they often host Sunday night dinners for their friends (not shown on these pages is the grand piano that we had craned in through a window so that he could play on these wonderful evenings). We thus returned the apartment to a more formal layout, one that encouraged the owners' flair for entertaining.

Thankfully, the bones were there—including beautiful high ceilings—so we didn't have to make any structural changes and instead focused on the cosmetic and function-driven elements of each room. This young couple longed for an apartment like the homes where they had grown up: classic and traditional. It was vital to me that upon completion, the apartment would not only embody this elegance but also reflect the youth of this young couple who live beautifully. Unexpected colors aided us in that endeavor, bringing in a sense of boldness and playfulness to complement the antiques that were part of their collection.

A fanciful foyer is the warmest possible welcome, setting the tone for gracious living within.

In the formal living room, we planned a timeless, symmetrical layout with traditional fabrics, then added hand-blocked batik wallpaper, a lot of black (which grounds the space), and touches of bottle-green velvet and leopard print. Altogether the space looks classical yet fresh. Multiple seating areas ensure maximum functionality; when you're hosting fifteen or twenty people, you want your guests to be able to break off into smaller tête-à-tête zones without having to rearrange your floor plans to accommodate the more intimate groupings. This room exemplifies that flexibility. It's also home to some of my favorite light fixtures ever: the pair of 1930s French sconces that now hang above the mantel. Their crystal rods had to be installed one by one, in a specific numbered order, to fit within the half-round of each fixture. I did it myself, barely breathing, because it felt like I was defusing a tiny French bomb!

PAGE 120: The homeowner's Peter Beard artwork has pride of place in the living room. OPPOSITE: To perfect the entry hall's original green floral wallpaper, which we all adored, we painted the surrounding woodwork and doors a luminescent cream. The painted tole lantern adds to the room's *Secret Garden* effect.

We maximized the space in the living room by tucking plush benches on either side of the fireplace. The jute rug underfoot and elements of black stave off a feeling of preciousness.

BLACK AS AN ACCENT

Many people fear black, in part because it feels like a commitment. I would say that it's quite the opposite. Black can have a calming, grounding effect in a room; I even painted our kitchen in it (Benjamin Moore Onyx)! It also tends to make all the other pieces in the room more interesting by juxtaposition. And frankly, there is a reason why women wear black—it's very flattering. Black paint can also conceal a multitude of sins on an inexpensive piece of furniture. For me, as someone who uses a lot of color, it is the world's best neutral—even better than white.

If you're nervous to dip your toe into jet black, try experimenting with a storage piece or coffee table. Those are nice ways to dabble in this shade as they can be layered with lighter objects like books and picture frames to break up the expanse of the color itself. It's worth noting that pure black doesn't exist; every black has color feedback in it, and you really need to be thoughtful about the undercurrent of the color tones with which you are combining it. This particular room has very warm color tones, so we needed to pair it with a cooler, stronger black so the tones didn't fight one another.

OPPOSITE: The sconces were originally made in France during the 1930s yet still wonderfully modern today. ABOVE: The bottle-green sofa and plants aplenty bring life to the room.

When in doubt about a decorative arrangement, opt for balance. It's a design tool that has lasted for centuries for a reason.

We did keep one decorative finish from the previous owners: the hand-painted green wallcovering in the entry hall, which we all agreed added such a sense of beauty and tranquility to the space that we would've been proud to have chosen it ourselves. We did alter the surrounding woodwork, which was originally a much brighter white and not high gloss, because we wanted the space to feel warmer and to have less contrast. In the center of it all is a skirted table with fringes that provides a quiet contrast against the wood parquet floors.

Soon after we started this project, the couple announced that they were expecting their first child—so exciting!—and we quickly dreamed up a nursery for the little boy, choosing a customized Marthe Armitage wallcovering in a warm saffron yellow (deeper than traditional nursery hues) and mixing in soft, turquoise-blue accents. As a nod to the traditional nursery tropes, we found antique prints of classic British cars and framed them in a grid above the daybed. New parents with sleepless babes need all the tranquility they can muster, so we conjured up a primary bedroom that feels like a soothing retreat. The canopy bed takes center stage with its inverted pleats and a padded headboard in a Rosa Bernal fabric. The hint of chocolate brown keeps the fabric from feeling too feminine.

PAGE 128: When reupholstering the clients' inherited nineteenth-century English dining chairs to make them more playful, we employed a different fabric—a chartreuse performance velvet—on the chair fronts. PAGE 129: Just a bit of gingham brings a carefree and breezy touch that lightens the mood. The curtains here are made of a double silk mohair velvet and weigh about forty-five pounds! OPPOSITE: It took us a while to land on this hand-painted platinum leaf de Gournay wallpaper in the formal dining room, but I'm so glad we did. It has incredible reflectivity that casts this treasure trove of antique pieces in a gorgeous light.

OPPOSITE: We used two similar handmade batik patterns, albeit in different scales, on the walls and pleated shade, which results in a layered yet cohesive feeling. ABOVE: In the kitchen, we brought in a leather corner banquette to echo the natural textures in the living room. The pendant light fixture above the cerused oak table was custom-made with a pattern, so it would feel very welcoming when it's on. Casa Gusto customized the frames for the botanical prints by pulling in hues from the surrounding cooking area.

ABOVE: As soon as I saw this room, I was obsessed with painting the woodwork a deep oxblood, which we then matched with the hard-wearing leather ottoman. OPPOSITE: The pleated lampshades are made of raw silk, which gives the Robert Kime pattern on the sofa an even more interesting texture. Note the jib door to the powder room that we wallpapered then trimmed with the same shade of oxblood as the woodwork.

This couple is lucky to have inherited wonderful family pieces, such as the nineteenth-century English table and chairs that we placed in the dining room. We upholstered the latter with chartreuse performance velvet on the chairbacks and a print on the seat, giving the traditional silhouette a bit more exuberance. Hand-painted de Gournay wallpaper in reflective platinum leaf and an antique, mercury glass and crystal chandelier bring in a sense of airiness. The opposite atmosphere was our aim in the nearby library, where we created a cocoon-like environment, painting the woodwork and shelves a deep oxblood and sheathing the walls in a small-scale tribal wallpaper from Schumacher. If I could marry a fabric, it would be the Robert Kime velvet that we used to upholster the library's sofa. It is comprised of muted shades of purples, blues, and dusky pinks, and the weave is sumptuous and decadent. Incidentally, that sofa—along with the sofa in the living room—had to be put on top of the carriage of the freight elevator to make their grand entrance into this apartment. I think it's fair to say that New Yorkers, and their erstwhile designers, look at logistical complexities like this as opportunities to prove our ingenuity.

Our clients longed for a canopy bed in the primary bedroom for a very serene, peaceful setting. This custom version has a padded headboard for comfort and a plethora of inverted pleats so you can admire the Rosa Bernal fabric from all angles. We installed hand-knotted, wall-to-wall carpet throughout their suite; it is luxurious and warm underfoot and provides continuity for the eye.

ABOVE: Every primary bedroom needs a conversation area for a morning cuppa and after-work chats. OPPOSITE: The Rosa Bernal fabric is a pale green-blue, but it has a bit of masculine chocolate brown in it. It allowed the bed to take center stage for a transporting experience.

ABOVE: This Marthe Armitage wallpaper is one of my all-time favorites—a happy yellow that's perfect for this little boy's nursery. OPPOSITE: We wanted to introduce blues as a secondary hue with turquoise lampshades and throw pillows. The art pieces above the twin daybed are prints of vintage cars that we purchased from an antique dealer—still a nod to boyhood but not as expected as, say, monster trucks.

CHAPTER FIVE

FEARLESS STYLE

I t's a rare privilege for a designer to work with a client who completely trusts their aesthetic vision, so much so that she is willing to follow their lead on most of the design direction and creative choices. This amazing woman—a Bedford local who often popped into our shop—had a lot of faith in the creative process from the very beginning. This freedom allowed for results that pushed the envelope: unusual color combinations and dramatic statement moments in an otherwise more traditional, architecturally specific home. Even before we began this project, I'd loved her home for years; it was part of a historic house tour that I'd participated in years previously, when it was inhabited by the previous owners, and I'd been dreaming about its potential ever since.

My client brought me onto the project during the final stages of planning an addition that would allow the house to better suit her growing family, including an expanded kitchen, mudroom, larger upstairs bedrooms, and closets. It was ideal timing, in that we were able to assist in reconceptualizing existing rooms and help to define the parameters and scope of the addition. The renovation aimed to embrace light and brightness where we could, because many rooms in the previous iteration of the home were quite dark. For instance, the family room was paneled in so much mahogany that it felt like a different genre entirely from the airy, high-ceilinged entryway. We reimagined this room, with nary a

PREVIOUS PAGE: A few modern touches—such as the subtly graphic wallcovering and vaguely Sputnik-like chandelier—balance more traditional choices in the entry. OPPOSITE: When my client bought this home, the family room was a bit dreary, as it was paneled in dark mahogany. We transformed it with decorative faux bois wall paint in a more easy-to-live-with cream. ABOVE: An abstract-printed grass cloth on the walls provides an interesting but not obtrusive backdrop in the foyer.

A jolt of contrast brings energy to a room as well as a note of the unexpected that makes a room feel curated and collected over time.

look back, by decoratively painting the mahogany a pale cream faux bois that brought in the sense of light and space evident in other areas of the home. Some clients might have balked at that change, but the previous wood felt so dark and oppressive, a stain on an otherwise sunny layout. The new wall treatment improved the tenor of the room while keeping its exposed grain texture, connecting it to the adjacent spaces.

This client is a fabulous cook and loves to entertain, so having a kitchen with an impressive footprint that allows family and friends to gather around while she's whipping up gourmet meals was very important. The island is eight feet long and topped with a 3½-inch-thick marble slab, and behind the sink, casement windows in a dark gray-black frame the verdant views into the gardens. We were intentional in our desire for nothing in this room to feel like it had "just been done," so that it could coexist with the historical nature of the house; case in point is the antique French chandelier hung above the island. We installed an abstract-printed grass cloth on the walls in the entryway that is both visually interesting and quiet enough to allow for bolder flourishes elsewhere, such as the antique turquoise Sputnik-style light fixture, Moroccan rug, and leopard settee.

We got even more playful in the living room, which is very traditional and large in scale at twenty-eight feet by seventeen feet. I'd been dying to combine

PREVIOUS PAGES AND OPPOSITE: When I first suggested chartreuse window treatments and pale pink walls, my client was a bit aghast: "In a million years I would never have done this." But they reflect her lovely, warm personality. Layering rugs can help a room feel even more welcoming. Hanging oil paintings on the front of bookshelves is a fresh approach that adds to the collected ambience.

pale peach walls and chartreuse taffeta window treatments for years, and my client indulged me. The paint color was a labor of love; of all the custom lacquer colors we've ever done, this took the longest to achieve the perfect hue and tonality. The space gets both morning and afternoon lights, so any color on the walls changes throughout the day. We were determined that it be a subtle peachy pink in daylight and then become richer and deeper as evening falls. At certain points during this process, I have no doubt that my painter, who listened patiently as I asked for more ochre or more white to be added to the mix, might've fantasized extensively about dumping one of the test gallons over my head, but he, and we, persevered, and it was worth it. As soon as the color and the curtains went up, it felt right: fresh and young and vibrant and unexpected, with the bonus of making the sprawling space feel more intimate. My client has an incredible art collection from her family and is herself a great collector, with many wonderful pieces to choose from. Hung on the wall, her oil paintings might have skewed the room too traditional, so we hung them on the bookcases—a much more youthful application that also brings them closer to the foreground.

One of my favorite rooms in this home is the media room, which we lovingly called "the Kasbah" while we were designing it. We wanted it to feel like the experience of walking into a Turkish tent, with its low, U-shaped custom sofa created to hug the contours of the room; bespoke Moorish-inspired ottoman; and a flurry of pillows. Warmed by one of my favorite Celerie Kemble Tortoise wallpapers, it's the ideal spot for this family to curl up for movie nights. And yet it's just as cinematic when all screens are off for an enchanting cocktail hour.

The dining room sits open to the entrance, so we wanted the walls to be relatively quiet—hence this beautiful Holland & Sherry wallcovering. The birdcage light fixture was a find from our antique dealer in Charleston, South Carolina, and has spectacular articulated pieces. Our custom cornice and octagonal dining table highlight its fanciful lines.

The slab of marble on the island's counter is 3½ inches thick; anything thinner would have felt insubstantial. I'm so glad we carried the marble up the backsplash; you can see the movement in the marble's striations, which draws your eye up the wall. The Christopher Farr wallcovering leading into the breakfast nook brings in bright happiness that mirrors the gardens beyond the windows.

UNUSUAL WALL FINISHES

ABOVE: Powder rooms are an opportunity for something escapist, such as this wallpaper with a slightly undersea effect. OPPOSITE: This sofa is actually U-shaped and wraps practically the entire room. Finished with Celerie Kemble Tortoise wallpaper and a custom Moorish-influenced ottoman, it's the type of den that, fair warning, your guests may never want to leave.

A lot of the homes that we work on are historic, and we've found that one of the most surefire ways to unify a room that might have developed disparate architectural styles over generations is to adorn everything in one interesting wallcovering. It grabs your attention in a way that allows everything else to recede.

In this space, a former owner had created a recessed niche for extra storage that sits behind a sofa. We decided to cover all the walls in Celerie Kemble Tortoise wallpaper for Schumacher. Not only does it have a great color variation within its pattern, but it is also a bit reflective, which unifies all those angles and corners and makes them feel as if they were all conceptualized at the same time.

Other unexpected wall finishes that we gravitate toward include faux bois decorative paint treatments—often with a bit of mica mixed in by our decorative painter to illuminate the wood "grain"—and silk strié, which we love because it's essentially a solid with texture that can obscure flaws in the walls. But really, tortoiseshell is my favorite. It's a very warm pattern and color, and it's also organic. We've said it before, but it bears repeating, there is no better designer than Mother Nature!

PREVIOUS PAGES: Our client is always amenable to making things feel special, so we took extra TLC with her primary suite, with its French Regency–era chandelier and palette of pale blues and corals. Black accents prevent it from reading too frilly. ABOVE: In soft shades of turquoise and pink, batiks and abstract polka dots give the daughter's room a boho yet quiet feeling. OPPOSITE: Custom window treatments give the son's room a fantastical look. FOLLOWING PAGES: The dining terrace sits off the formal living room. The furniture was intentionally weathered to look like it's been used for several seasons.

—CHAPTER SIX—

IN BLOOM

I t can sometimes take time to establish what I call "creative capital" with a client: the level of earned trust that allows you to take what might otherwise be considered high-risk design chances together. This couple have been good friends of mine for a long time, but they're also dreamy clients; together, we have many beautiful projects in our wake. Because we have worked with one another often and for so many years, we have developed a significant amount of creative capital and are able to explore the unexpected without the usual level of apprehension. That foundation forms the undercurrent of their second home, an 1880s Victorian that is the family's weekend retreat from their primary residence in Manhattan. It serves a multitude of functions: an epicenter for children's weekend activities, dinner parties with country friends, and a place to host their extended families when they come to visit (the last is always a particularly gratifying design endeavor).

The living room is a wonderful example of embracing multiple tasks in one cohesive space. The wife wanted it to feel light and airy: a place where they would be as comfortable doing puzzles on the Lucite table as they would be hosting guests for mah-jongg or cocktail hour. It's very considered and collected, in a way that suits

PAGE 163: When possible, window treatments should span floor to ceiling to draw the eye up in a space. PREVIOUS PAGES: Juliska Country Estate collection inspired the living room's dreamy color palette. The chairs are slipcovered in linen, which helps everyone relax; they can always be pulled off for cleaning. ABOVE: Including a few timeworn pieces can lend a newly redesigned space a sense of provenance. OPPOSITE: A mirror framed in Lucite adds to the airy sensibility in the living room.

The distressed Holland & Sherry leather on the sofa goes sumptuously with the plaid armchairs and cocoa-brown walls in my client's man cave. Symmetrical placement prevents the dimly lit room from looking disorganized or poorly considered.

THE HOME BAR

I like my bars to be like most things in my life: both decorative and functional. We as a team always walk a fine line in these spaces. I like to begin with an interesting material for the bar itself and, if it's possible, the backsplash. Amazing countertops are lovely, but for a home bar, they're often covered by objects. So if you continue them up the wall, the multidimensionality can be an effective design tool. We love antiqued mirrors, which can enlarge an often-petite space, and rainbow onyx. Here, the bar is agate, which creates an organic, randomly repeating pattern that clads not only the bar but climbs the backsplash.

To make it truly special, bring in a little bit of disparate light. I also prefer small lamps with interesting shades for warmth and decorative bar accessories, from ice buckets to embroidered cocktail napkins. I often ensure that actual bar "workhorse" items like stemware and glasses can be tucked within the cabinetry. The practicality of washing a glass before you use it each time because it's been sitting on an open shelf seems a trial not worth the libation. For parties, always have a bowl of something fresh and green, be it limes or just-snipped mint to muddle in cocktails. And while it's not very sexy, don't forget to design your space with power outlets in mind. An electrical outlet gives you the option of whirring up something fabulously frothy and potentially frozen, such as a jalapeño margarita on Cinco de Mayo.

OPPOSITE: Blue agate slabs form this attractive bar counter and backsplash, and pop against the high-gloss cabinetry in deep chocolate. Brass pulls add shimmer in low light. ABOVE: Antique architectural drawings add a sense of history.

Hosting events in surprising spaces kicks the fun up a notch and serves as an icebreaker.

the natural world just beyond the big, open windows. This is a different approach from the one we took in their city apartment, where interiors are more buttoned-up. Here, we opted for finishes that can handle children running in from the pool without worry. It still speaks to their high level of style and aesthetic, but everyone can remain nonplussed. They're here to unwind and relax from hectic city life after all, not fret about a blotch of something unidentifiable on the silk!

The husband had a special request for a space of his own here, a de facto man cave. Because much of the house reads as more feminine, we happily indulged him, designing a masculine hideaway with British gentleman's clubs as our muse. Chocolate-brown grass cloth immediately warmed the walls, while a custom sofa in distressed blue Holland & Sherry leather is a plump perch to sink into for a Rangers game (and, incidentally, fairly waterproof—which is handy when a friend gets raucous after a goal and spills their drink). The bar was a place where our stockpiled creative capital paid big. Rather than doing something standard-issue, we designed the counter and backsplash with blue agate slabs that pop beautifully against the high-gloss, deep chocolate cabinetry. I lost a few nights of sleep as they were being installed, because agate is a porous material and can be tricky to fabricate, but it came out perfectly. He is also an oenophile, so we created a wine cellar just off the

We went through countless different elevations while planning the white oak wine cellar, but it was worth the effort. It's a charming and unexpected place to host friends and family for a tipple. The moody, gleaming chandelier and elegant table tell visitors at a glance that this is more than a purely functional space.

Gold onyx countertops and plenty of sconces, pendant lights, and other decorative fixtures add to the warm, inviting glow of the wine cellar. Underfoot, a polished concrete floor has an industrial effect that will always feel modern.

ABOVE: Like kitchen sinks, desks are practically made for placement before a window; it's wonderful to glance up from your work to see a flitting bird or leaves dancing in the wind. OPPOSITE: The peach-pink Murano chandelier is a note of sweetness in the guest suite, where Casa Branca wallcovering makes the most of the eaves.

ABOVE, CLOCKWISE FROM TOP LEFT: Small, black details ground the color palette. Botanical prints are classic for good reason. We upped the ante on bedside reading lamps by matching this one to the headboard. Long live the spindle chair, especially covered in rainbow-sherbert-striped taffeta. OPPOSITE: Baskets and handwoven rugs create a layer of earthy texture.

OPPOSITE: Orchids can be hard to take care of, but the TLC you give them is worth it; they bring so much life to a room. ABOVE, CLOCKWISE FROM TOP LEFT: Marbleized lampshades add a cool factor. There's something endlessly delicious about peach Murano glass. A note of chinoiserie brings an aura of history. Ebonized pieces are important in a room with a pastel palette.

Even mudrooms can be magical. There can be so much beauty when form and function are both served in equal measure.

man cave that would cause any sommelier's heart to skip a beat. We designed it to accomplish two things: store his extensive collection in an accessible way and be beautiful enough to host wine tastings or even a dinner party. The white oak shelving pairs marvelously with the gold onyx counters. We also used decorative sconces and pendants for mood lighting to ensure that the space felt intimate as opposed to utilitarian. The polished concrete floor was poured twice to achieve the perfect color and finish, proving once again that the devil is in the little details! Our clients are thrilled with the room and the unusual materials. So while it's a bit chilly—all the better for cellaring wine— it's a frequent destination for entertaining.

One of my favorite spaces in this home is the guest suite, and I'm not alone; I'm told that visitors will often fight over who gets to stay in this room, which is the ultimate goal of any guest suite. We used a neutral wallpaper from Casa Branca that we love, because it's visually interesting yet muted enough to handle art and other strong design elements, such as the coral-pink Murano chandelier. While using soft pale pinks, creams, and racing greens, we were mindful to bring in a touch of black furniture to ground the room. Otherwise, it may have looked like a sorbet sundae: delicious but a note too sweet. Like the rest of the home, the resulting interior is exactly what anyone might dream of for a weekend respite. It's warm and welcoming, yes—and also utterly indulgent.

Because the mudroom is part of an addition to the main house, we were able to fully customize it. For example, we created detailed cubbies for each member of the family and upper bins for items that can be stored seasonally, like mittens and scarves. The floors are Pennsylvania bluestone in a herringbone pattern that makes the space feel even larger.

These parents presciently created a "bunk room" away from their primary suite so their children can host sleepovers out of earshot. Adding curtains to the bunks themselves makes them more useful; it's possible to draw them closed, turn your lamp on, and read into the night without disturbing your bunkmates.

ABOVE, CLOCKWISE FROM TOP LEFT: This is a new space, so we worked hard to introduce items from different eras. The Greek fret is iconic for a reason. Natural fibers and fringe deliver playfulness. Custom bolsters in a vintage-inspired motif bring the fun. OPPOSITE: Every window seat is also an opportunity for storage compartments. FOLLOWING PAGES: Sun-washed fabrics add to the settled-in feeling; we didn't want everything to feel like we just bought it yesterday.

—CHAPTER SEVEN—

WEEKEND BLISS

hen my clients purchased this 1960s house as a weekend and summer home, it had interesting light and a fantastic location but was somewhat devoid in the personality department. They wanted to introduce an element of whimsy from the moment you arrive, so we added some quirky but charming sheep in the entryway, as well as wallpaper that climbs the eaves, dark millwork to accentuate the doors, trims, and architectural details, and an Urban Electric pendant light in a darker hue that makes the most of the vaulted ceiling. To complement them all, we sourced an antique oil portrait with an air of gravitas, but the subject candidly has a glint in his eye that looks slightly mischievous.

In their voluminous, double-height living room, we hung a wallpaper that approximates driftwood and carried it all the way up into the eaves of the second floor. It's frequently the case that a room of this scale can feel like an austere white box, and the faux bois wall treatment settles the space in a warm, neutral fashion. During the renovation, we opened up the sunroom and kitchen for an open-concept floor plan that suited their weekend lifestyle. For urbanites on vacation from the city,

Consider bringing sculptures into an otherwise bare corner. The play on height provides tension and gives meaning to the space.

it felt right to lean into touches of the rustic that fit country life, such as the wooden chandelier and notes of chocolate brown for warmth. In the kitchen, a Moroccan rug and brass hardware provide contrast to the cool blue tones of the cabinetry, and the stools are de facto art pieces as their negative space is as interesting as their positive space when perceived from the living area.

To fulfill its purpose, the sunroom needed to feel lounge-like, the perfect spot to curl up with the *New York Times* Sunday crossword, with easy access to the garden for indoor-outdoor living that's delightful in warmer months. We were gratified by our client's support of our idea to paint the window sash an inky black. The transformation framed their garden in a way that makes it look like living art beyond the glass. Adding to the effect are the textiles in the room, which we selected for their earthy, even slightly muddy, undertones. They're new but still somehow manage to convey an English country home ambience, as if they were inherited rather than purchased. We custom designed the two poufs so that they could be easily pushed together or separated, depending on the size of the gathering. Their round shape

PAGE 190: Ever since Les Lalanne glamorized sheep sculptures in the 1960s, they've brought instant charm and are especially fitting in a country house. OPPOSITE: An inky trim color—Farrow & Ball Hague Blue—gives this home a less-suburban feel. Wooden sculptures turn an underused corner into a moment. FOLLOWING PAGES: We warmed up the double-height living room with faux bois wallpaper.

ABOVE: In the kitchen, sculptural stools help define the space; in relief against the dark blue of the island, they become art. On blonde oak floors, the Beni Ourain rug pops. OPPOSITE: Country homes practically beg for window seats: an idyllic nook for whiling away an afternoon.

If you're lucky enough to have a view of nature, embrace it every way you can. Frame the view out a window with a strong color, or dramatic curtains.

provides a counterpoint to the angularity of the window framing and shiplap wall treatment.

For their primary bedroom, my clients asked for a space with Anglo-Indian influence. We started with a four-poster bed that we rendered less serious with light, warm accents. One of the first things we picked for this room was a Bennison textile, our hero fabric that has the richest palette of creams, charcoals, Delft blues, browns, and a mustard-ochre color and also walks a fine line between the feminine and the masculine. The punch of the ochre keeps the room from feeling too sedate and gives it a bit of a wink—not unlike the antique oil portrait of the gentleman with the subtly mischievous look from the entry: dignified but never taking oneself too seriously.

The sunroom couldn't be overly fancy because its doors slide open to the garden and wilderness beyond. My clients were initially resistant to painting the grand window jet black, but I'm glad we did; it perfectly frames the view. The duo of custom round ottomans helps break up all the lines in the room and are highly portable.

STYLING YOUR OWN HOME

ABOVE: We embraced an Anglo-Indian feeling in the primary suite, which inspired a lot of beautiful, natural textures that help counteract the interesting ceiling shape. OPPOSITE: The four-poster bed might feel serious if not for the Bennison textile we selected, which is light and warm in its palette of cream, charcoal brown, Delft blues, and even a whisper of zingy yellow.

Layering in those final finishing touches to your space—from decorative *objets* to books—is intensely personal, and I always consider the clients' preferences in advance as taste varies widely. For example, I personally can't stand the sight of a remote on my nightstand and always tuck it inside of an inlaid box. It's always right where I left it, and the box functions as a decorative element for the case piece that it rests on. However, I know there are people who would be nervous if they couldn't see their remotes within reach at all times!

My maxim is that if you pick things that you are drawn to, your choices can never be wrong. Consider your interests, including your passions, collections, and preferences. Do you respond to architectural engravings? Are you a person who loves watercolors? Do you want to have a chair with a little lumbar pillow?

I've found that I require multiple sources of light in varying wattages, depending on their function. I prefer a dimmable sconce for reading over my bed and brighter wattage on dressers where I may need to ascertain the difference between black and blue, an increasingly difficult task as I get older. I always make sure to find a place for my greenery, whether it be a brass cachepot or an interesting wide-weave seagrass basket. Above all, I love to be surrounded by the meaningful objects that I have collected over the years, many of which hold memories and will form the backdrop for more to come.

ABOVE, CLOCKWISE FROM TOP LEFT: This bathroom is just off the library, and its green glass tiles add to the bibliophile effect. Special, unexpected pieces are vital for giving personality to a home. The powder room near the entry is a jewel box. Turkish tiles and a claw-foot tub add a sense of worldly enchantment to the guest bath. OPPOSITE: Natural textures can supply warmth to a white-on-white bath.

OPPOSITE: One of the first things we picked for the guest suite was Michael Smith's abstract striped wallpaper, which is an unusual combination of oxblood, brown, and cool blue. It's not as simplistic as a basic stripe and still brings a sense of verticality to the room. ABOVE: A jute rug is my favorite natural texture underfoot, particularly for a home used mainly in the summer.

CHAPTER EIGHT

A MANOR OF SPEAKING

This Georgian Revival home in St. Louis, Missouri, is one of my favorite projects that we have done to date—in part because we became so close to this wonderful family over the course of the work and in part because our clients had amassed an incredible art collection even before we began. It was a true gift to collaborate with these clients, who informed the design concepts but were also so trusting of the design process and our ideas that they allowed us to do some of our finest work and to be continually inspired by—and hopefully rewarded—their artistic faith in us.

My clients found me the old-fashioned way, through press clippings from magazines in which we'd been published. She had been saving images she liked on Instagram and from editorial features, and she told us that when it became time to choose with whom they would work on this house, she pulled her inspiration images together and discovered something prophetic: "Even though they were all from different homes, I realized that nine out of ten of them were designed by you."

We were lucky enough to come aboard during this project's nascent phase, just as Ferguson & Shamamian Architects had begun its plans for the home's addition and rebuild. That's an amazing luxury for any design firm, because it allows them to inform many of the interior architectural choices in a way that is reflective of

Accents in earthy browns and jet blacks
can tone down feral hues, like vermilion,
in patent leather no less.

their design concepts. Ferguson & Shamamian had designed this home when it was originally built for the first owners in the early 1990s. Every family uses a home differently, which demands a tailored approach, and everyone on this team felt strongly that the architecture is most effective when it serves both the function and the form. To this end, our clients longed to expand the home's footprint to reflect their modern lifestyle, including a kitchen, mudroom, gym, family room, and an extension of the rear terrace, all of which needed to make sense when viewed within the larger architectural envelope.

It was important to all of us that we honor the formality and graciousness of the home, so in the foyer we enlisted our decorative painter to create a classic Harlequin pattern on the floor that was consistent with the architectural style. Brunschwig & Fils sage wallcovering is grass cloth but very elevated: it's a repeating chinoiserie-inspired scene embroidered by hand. Because this hall is very much a central artery to various other formal entertaining spaces, it was vital to create a sense of arrival. To meet this goal, we designed an oversize settee in a printed Bennison silk, and its cushion was boxed in a soft, dusty-pink silk fringe. Down-filled silk cushions can sometimes settle into a "droopy drawers" effect, so we did quite a few sit tests to ensure this was appropriately filled. It makes a luxuriously comfortable place to rest and pull on your loafers!

PAGE 207: The gracious entrance called for elegance at every turn, as emphasized by the wallcovering: a hand-embroidered grass cloth. PREVIOUS PAGES: The clients' trove of Imari porcelain and the Matisse painting hung over the mantel inspired the living room's color palette of soothing Swedish blue grays and rusty reds. OPPOSITE: Personal collections bring a deeper meaning to a room, such as these boxes accumulated by the homeowner's father. The silk window treatments provide a refined moment in a room that's otherwise not too precious.

The oxblood wallcovering in the dining room spoke to me instantly, in part because it's painted on distressed tea paper; it feels in keeping with the home's architecture. We designed and built the arched alcoves specifically to hold the clients' pairs of French antique mirrors and consoles.

ABOVE: Arches are forever chic; they give every passageway an aura of stately grandeur. OPPOSITE: The first thing purchased for this home was this antique French bibliothèque. It has the amazing ability to adapt along with the lives around it. The interior was already that gorgeous color, which is a lovely complementary hue to the treillage we eventually built in the room around it.

In the formal living room, a piece by Matisse, now hanging over the mantel, dictated the color choices employed in this room. Originally, the space was a classic room lined with midtone oak that felt a bit traditional; now it's a soothing, decoratively striated Swedish blue gray, with deep teal blues and rusty corals offset by Gustavian-era patent leather chairs that keep the room from feeling too precious. The silk curtains we selected are a refined moment. We loved the material so much that we upholstered one of the sofas with it and added trapunto quilting for a three-dimensional effect. No detail was overlooked, even down to the multicolored fringe on the custom ottoman, chosen for its ability to pull every single color in the room's hero silk fabric into its motif.

While the millwork throughout this home was an important consideration to everyone on the team, the treillage in the breakfast room was my baby, and we worked closely with our amazing partners at Ferguson & Shamamian to ensure

I knew early on that we would adorn the breakfast room in a traditional French treillage. Facing the verdant lawns, with abundant daylight bouncing off the antiqued mirror backing, it's an ideal place to begin the day—just add croissants.

ABOVE, CLOCKWISE FROM TOP LEFT: The bar is next to the dining room and connects to the living room and kitchen. Roman shades give the beautiful woodwork its star moment. Black onyx counters are palpably glamorous. Antiqued-mirror cabinet insets give a handsome shimmer. OPPOSITE: Having sourced the slab of black onyx in New York, I had a very tense few days waiting for it to arrive on a truck. It finally made it and was well worth the wait. The bar sink is a hammered brass that also catches the light.

POWERFUL POWDER ROOMS

Powder rooms are essentially the only rooms in your home that are designed entirely for guests, and they're often very small in scale. These two specifics allow you a lot more freedom than you have in other spaces to indulge in interesting textural choices and wallcoverings. We call this the "jewel box" effect, because it should feel similar to opening a small box to find it intricately lined and filled with miniature treasures. In general, these spaces don't require much storage; it's essentially a quick stop to powder your nose and freshen up, and that's to your advantage.

Because powder rooms are often located in the front of the home, either adjacent to an entertaining space or just off the foyer, they should be as decoratively pleasing as your other gathering spaces. One of my favorite transportive approaches is to sheathe them in a scenic wallpaper that both tells a story and adds depth to a small room. Countertop space is minimal, so you can splurge on something especially lavish for your vanity, such as pink onyx. In keeping with the jewel box concept, lighting can be a bit moodier, which opens up a world of antique and vintage fixtures. Anything that twinkles is a perennial favorite, and I like all my powder room fixtures to be dimmable. Everyone looks better under the glow of antique mercury glass from a hôtel particulier in Paris!

OPPOSITE: Topped in pink onyx, the chinoiserie dresser-turned-vanity is as fanciful as it is useful. ABOVE: Because this powder room is among the first things you see when you walk in the front door, we were determined to make it beautiful. FOLLOWING PAGES: Custom, cerused-oak cabinets by Ferguson & Shamamian Architects put the clients' china on display.

ABOVE: We tucked a coffee bar within the butler's pantry and added a decoratively painted runner to the floor, which is highly functional in a room that gets a lot of foot traffic. OPPOSITE: Soane Britain pendants are a light, textural counterpoint to the weight of the island.

OPPOSITE: Mudrooms are utilitarian, but that doesn't mean they can't be attractive. I love the wallpaper we selected, which is a warm tobacco hue with icy blue gray and a mere murmur of aubergine. ABOVE: We designed decorative cutouts that allow air to flow into the coat closets—handy after a drizzly walk.

Contemporary artworks inject a needed juxta-position into traditional spaces, turning softer patterns and classical lines on their head.

that our vision came to life. We echoed the architecture of the columns and terrace within its patterns, so that the repetition felt seamless and consistent within the two spaces. We were fortunate to be able to design the room—both structurally and in regard to the treillage—around the very first piece that we purchased for the project, an antique French bibliothèque from Casa Gusto, my dear friends in Palm Beach, which instilled a sense of age and history to an otherwise "new" space.

We endeavored to achieve the same level of artistic detail in the bedrooms. The primary needed to feel restful and serene, so we began by hanging a hand-embroidered wallpaper with a raised, three-dimensional geometric per-spective. We added subtle interest to the Bennison silk window treatments by running a Schumacher silk-taffeta pleated-ruffle detail along their leading edge. The en suite bath is a testament to the power of mixed materials, with its rainbow onyx, hand-painted rose gold leaf wallpaper with faux bois wood graining, and Murano sconces. The last have a beautiful texture to their glass that produces an incredibly flattering light.

Indeed, there's no law that prevents our most functional spaces from be-ing exquisitely stunning, and we referenced that idea in even the most practi-cal spaces in this home. Our aim with the mudroom, for example, was to make it feel decorative even though it needed to serve a utilitarian function. The

OPPOSITE: Just one modern art piece—such as this one by Robert Motherwell—can bring a room with otherwise traditional choices into the present. And I love the Soane Britain light fixtures in this family room. FOLLOWING PAGES: The ceilings here are the highest throughout the entire home; we warmed the space with a hand-blocked batik floral.

ABOVE: The clients' marble urns were practically tailor-made to flank the fireplace in the family room. They're so heavy that I can only carry their lids! OPPOSITE: We selected a sofa with one long seat cushion for comfort and upholstered it in a tobacco brown.

floors are a durable Pennsylvania bluestone, and the sophisticated wallcovering plays off this palette, with its rich tobacco browns, icy blue grays, and a hint of aubergine. Above them all are laylights designed by Ferguson & Shamamian to withstand the cold, harsh winters of St. Louis while still allowing this room to be bathed in natural light.

The powder room just off the foyer, too, required a careful approach as it's one of the first rooms on display when you enter the home. We transformed an antique chinoiserie case piece into a sink vanity and topped its curves with delicate pink onyx. We rendered the walls in a subtle grisaille wallcovering to avoid overwhelming the petite space and to consider the fact that there is already significant color in that section of the home. This strategy proved my favorite design adage that a moment of quiet relief often renders bold colors more interesting.

Looking back, the dining room may have been our biggest lesson in trusting the creative process. While our clients did not have many specific requests related to color, they were not enamored with purple. Therefore, when I showed them the hand-painted de Gournay oxblood wallpaper that we hoped to install in this space, they were a bit nervous—understandably, as purple and oxblood are closely related on the color wheel. But with great risk comes great reward, and we are immensely pleased that at the conclusion of this project, this was the space they ended up loving the most. Combining the wallpaper with acid-chartreuse leather upholstery on our Regency-style chairs and a bold Patterson Flynn abaca rug ensured that the final product feels elegant and thoughtful but not overly formal. It is always our greatest privilege to create a perfect space such as this to celebrate life's milestones.

OPPOSITE: For the upstairs hallway, I designed these two settees and had them upholstered in an exquisite Pierre Frey fabric. Because you're primarily perceiving them from the sides, it was crucial to me that the silhouette have beautiful curves. We call it "the Brittany Special." Relaxed braided cotton trim and an artwork by Robert Motherwell complete the eye candy effect.

Raised, three-dimensional silk wallpaper is especially serene in the primary suite. The ruffle of the window treatments' leading edge is a silk taffeta pinstripe from Schumacher, but we ran it horizontally for added interest.

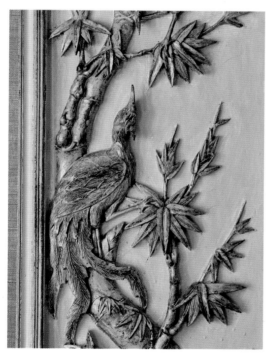

OPPOSITE: The custom shades on the reading lamps were handmade for us in France. They're like jewelry for your lighting. The bed linens, too, are custom and as intricately scalloped as a peacock. ABOVE, CLOCKWISE FROM TOP LEFT: These sconces catch the light beautifully after dark. Ruffles are always refined. A contemplative reading nook. Antique carved wall panels visually anchor the bed.

Hand-painted rose gold leaf wallpaper topped with a faux bois effect marries well with Gold rainbow onyx and Calacatta gold marble in the primary bathroom. The Murano sconces are incredibly flattering, partly because the glass is so vividly textured.

ABOVE: A skirted stool at the vanity is a timeless, feminine perch. OPPOSITE: Allowing the Roman shade to droop a bit has a graceful effect that's lovely in an en suite.

OPPOSITE: The primary suite's sitting room walks a fine line between masculine and feminine. The husband's collection of duck decoys found their roost here. ABOVE: Our drapery crew spent five days on-site building these sophisticated valances to perfectly fit the molding profile. The wallpaper is a textured grass cloth printed with paisleys from Elizabeth Eakins.

OPPOSITE: We designed the son's room to be so handsome that it will stand the test of time. Someday when he has left the nest and returns home for a visit, it will still feel age appropriate. This is a family of boaters, so we took a nautical inspiration for his bedside lamps. ABOVE: I designed this wool wingback chair to accommodate his very tall frame.

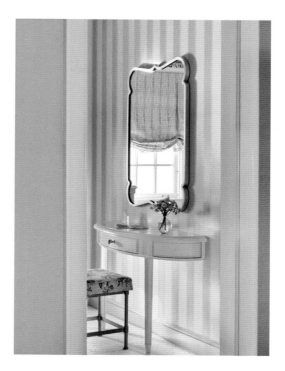

OPPOSITE: Navy blue and bottle green add interest to a girl's room while playing well with the peach grass cloth. ABOVE, CLOCKWISE FROM TOP LEFT: The clients' young daughter has a warm, feminine energy and wanted her room to follow suit. Every girl needs a vanity tailored just to her. Moorish-inspired floor tiles grace her bathroom. Pierre Frey wallpaper combines the room's color palette of pinks and greens.

OPPOSITE AND ABOVE: We were all incredibly excited to design this craft room. It was the first we've ever done, and we were determined to make it amazing. This Pierre Frey wallpaper was ideal for the space. It's effervescent and has the added benefit of being wipeable vinyl; in short, finger paint has met its match. PAGE 253: Pierre Frey wallpaper adorns my daughter's room.

ACKNOWLEDGMENTS

I would like to thank the following people, whose support and friendship mean the world to me:

My parents, Libby and David Horn, from whom I get my style, who trained my eye, believed in my potential, and have loved me endlessly through the best and worst of times, and my brother, Brecht, who always makes me laugh and is a tremendous uncle.

Kathryn Leardo—forever "Katie the Greaty"—whose skill, patience, and sense of humor make our work feel like play.

Alexandra Drucker, my adopted sister, who has been cheering me on for twenty-five years and who is the best friend one could ever ask for.

Alessandra Branca, whose wise counsel and support informed so many of my choices in this industry.

My daughters, Charlotte and Gigi, who fill my life with love and laughter and their father, Matt Bromley, for his friendship and encouragement of all my endeavors, and Paula Gomez who has loved my children like a second mother for the entirety of their lives.

Jill Cohen, my mother of dragons without whom this book would still be a dream and whose advice is given freely and often and whose friendship means so much to me.

Cris Briger, Charles Peed, and Augie Briger—my Casa Gusto family, who adopted me into their loving and beautiful world and continue to inspire me with their tremendous talent, depth of knowledge, and boundless creative energy.

To NML, for your wonderful, patient advice, and for reminding me how lovely it is to be happy.

Barbara Webb, whose style and wit were a fixture in my youth and who taught me that animal print is always a neutral.

Michael Boodro, Clinton Smith, Amy Astley, Steele Marcoux, Robert Rufino, Hadley Keller, Jill Waage, Carolyn Englefield, Pamela Jaccarino, and Cynthia Frank for publishing my work.

My Rizzoli family—Charles Miers, Kathleen Jayes, Doug Turshen, Steve Turner, Kathryn O'Shea-Evans, Melissa Powell, and Lizzy Hyland—for making this dream of a book into a hardbound reality.

Annie Schlechter and Paul Fittipaldi, whose talented photography so beautifully captures my work and whose sense of humor makes even the longest of shoot days a joy.

To all our amazing vendors, partner workrooms, and tradespeople, whose dedication to their craft makes every project possible and whose commitment to excellence inspires us. And a very special thank you to Ana Muralles and Claudia Gomez, who have been by our sides since the beginning and who make even the impossible seem simple.

And finally, thank you to all my friends, employees, and, most importantly, clients without whose support and trust in me, this book would have never been possible.

RESOURCES

ART/ACCESSORIES:

Kate Bellin Contemporary
www.katebellin.com

Katonah Architectural Hardware:
www.katonahhardware.com

KRB: www.krbnyc.com

Luxholdups: www.luxholdups.com

Mirror Home: www.mirrorhome.com

Rosi de Ruig: www.rosideruig.co.uk/

ANTIQUES:

1stDibs: www.1stdibs.com

The Antique and Artisan Gallery:
www.theantiqueandartisangallery.com

Casa Gusto: www.getthegusto.com

Chairish: www.chairish.com

Gerald Bland: www.geraldblandinc.com

John Rosselli & Associates: www.johnrosselli.com

Patricia's Gallery: www.patriciasgallerywpb.com

ARCHITECTS:

Ferguson & Shamamian Architects:
www.fergusonshamamian.com

BATH FIXTURES:

P. E. Guerin: www.peguerin.com

Waterworks: www.waterworks.com/us_en

CONTRACTORS:

Higginbotham Custom Homes & Renovation:
@higginbothambros

NYC Fine Finishes: www.nycfinefinishes.com

Taconic Builders: www.taconicbuilders.com

DECORATIVE PAINTERS:

Mary Meade Evans @marymeadeevans

Shelly Denning @shellypaint

FABRIC/WALLCOVERINGS:

Bennison Fabrics: www.bennisonfabrics.com

Carolina Irving Textiles: www.carolinairvingtextiles.com

Casa Branca: www.casabranca.com/collections/fabric

Chelsea Textiles: www.chelseatextiles.com/us

Claremont Furnishing: www.claremontfurnishing.com

Clarence House: www.clarencehouse.com

Cowtan & Tout: www.cowtan.com

de Gournay: www.degournay.com

Décor de Paris: www.decordeparis.com

Elizabeth Dow: www.elizabethdow.com

Farrow & Ball: www.farrow-ball.com/us/

Fermoie: www.fermoie.com/product-category/fabric

Fine Paints of Europe: www.finepaintsofeurope.com

Gracie: www.graciestudio.com

Hartmann&Forbes: www.hartmannforbes.com

Holland & Sherry: www.hollandandsherry.com

John Rosselli & Associates: www.johnrosselli.com

Kathryn M. Ireland: www.kathrynireland.com

Lisa Fine Textiles: www.lisafinetextiles.com

Nicholas Herbert: www.nicholasherbert.com

Peter Fasano: www.peterfasano.com

Phillip Jeffries: www.phillipjeffries.com

Pierre Frey: www.pierrefrey.com/en

Quadrille: www.quadrillefabrics.com

Robert Kime: www.robertkime.com

Rogers & Goffigon: www.rogersandgoffigon.com

Rosa Bernal: www.therosabernalcollection.com

Schumacher: www.schumacher.com

Soane Britain: www.soane.co.uk

Thibaut: www.thibautdesign.com

ZAK+FOX: www.zakandfox.com

FURNITURE:

Currey & Company: www.curreyandcompany.com

Dunes and Duchess: www.dunesandduchess.com

George Smith: www.georgesmith.com

Hollywood at Home: www.hollywoodathome.com

Keith Fritz: www.keithfritz.com

McKinnon and Harris: www.mckinnonharris.com

Mecox: www.mecox.com

O. Henry House: www.ohenryhouseltd.com

Yung Atelier: www.yungatelier.com

LIGHTING:

Christopher Spitzmiller: www.christopherspitzmiller.com

Coleen & Company: www.coleenandcompany.com

Galerie des Lampes: www.galeriedeslampes.com/front/presentation.php

Hector Finch: www.hectorfinch.com

illumé: www.illumenyc.com

Jamb: www.jamb.co.uk/us/lighting

Katie Leede and Company: www.katieleede.com

Lionsgate Antiques: www.lionsgateantiquesnyc.com

Niermann Weeks: www.niermannweeks.com

Visual Comfort: www.visualcomfort.com

LINENS:

D. Porthault: www.dporthaultparis.com

Leontine Linens: www.leontinelinens.com

Schweitzer Linen: www.schweitzerlinen.com

PASSEMENTERIES:

Décor de Paris: www.decordeparis.com

Samuel & Sons: www.samuelandsons.com/en

Travers: www.zimmer-rohde.com/en/brands/travers

RUGS:

Beauvais: www.beauvaiscarpets.com

Elizabeth Eakins: www.elizabetheakins.com

Fibreworks: www.fibreworks.com

From Jaipur with Love: www.fromjaipurwithloverugs.com

Merida: www.meridastudio.com

Patterson Flynn: www.pattersonflynn.com

Stark: www.starkcarpet.com

First published in the United States of America in 2025 by
Rizzoli International Publications, Inc.
49 West 27th Street
New York, NY 10001
www.rizzoliusa.com

Text: Kathryn O'Shea-Evans
Photography:
All photos by Annie Schlecter except:
Page 11: Shea Kastriner
Pages 163, 164–65, 167: Jane Beiles
Page 254: Carmel Brantley

Art Credits:
Page 68: Kikuo Saito, *Grasshopper*, 2012
Page 69: Cy Twombly, *Roman Notes I*, 1970 © Cy Twombly Foundation
Page 70: Sebastiaan Bremer, *Schoener Goetterfunken XXIX, "On their courses through the heavens" (Durch des Himmels prachtigen Plan)*, 2017
Page 70: Spencer Finch, *Paths through the studio 8/31/20-10/10/20 II*, 2020
Page 75: Agnes Barley, *Continuous Stroke*, 2021
Pages 76–77: Natasha Law, *Flowers, Red on Pink*, 2021
Page 85: Gray Malin, *Ladies Beach II, Nantucket*
Page 88: Agnes Barley, *Untitled Collage (Deconstructed Waves)*, 2021
Page 93: Agnes Barley, *Untitled Collage (Deconstructed Waves)*, 2009
Page 120: Peter Beard, Lion Pride, near Ndutu, Southern Serengetti, Tanzania, 1976 © 2024 The Estate of Peter Beard / Licensed by Artists Rights Society (ARS), New York
Page 207: Helen Frankenthaler, Snow Pines, 2004 © 2024 Helen Frankenthaler Foundation, Inc. / Artists Rights Society (ARS), New York / Pace Editions, Inc. / New York
Pages 208–209: Henri Matisse, Marie-José en robe jaune, c. 1950 © 2024 Succession H. Matisse / Artists Rights Society (ARS), New York
Page 233: Robert Motherwell, Hollow Men II, 1985-87/1988-89 © 2024 Dedalus Foundation, Inc. / Artists Rights Society (ARS), New York
Page 234: Robert Motherwell, Untitled, 1990 © 2024 Dedalus Foundation, Inc. / Artists Rights Society (ARS), NY
Page 247: Louise Nevelson, Double Imagery (diptych), 1967 © 2024 Estate of Louise Nevelson / Artists Rights Society (ARS), New York
Page 249: Kenneth Noland, Days and Nights, 2008 © 2024 The Kenneth Noland Foundation / Licensed by VAGA at Artists Rights Society (ARS), New York

Publisher: Charles Miers
Senior Editor: Kathleen Jayes
Design: Doug Turshen with Steve Turner
Production Manager: Rebecca Ambrose
Managing Editor: Lynn Scrabis

Developed in collaboration with Jill Cohen Associates

ISBN: 978-0-8478-4529-3
Library of Congress Control Number: 2024945540

Printed in China
2025 2026 2027 2028 / 10 9 8 7 6 5 4 3 2 1

Visit us online:
Instagram.com/RizzoliBooks
Facebook.com/RizzoliNewYork
X: @Rizzoli_Books
Youtube.com/user/RizzoliNY